Together

Poems by

Kaveri Patel

For Dori Ma. May your loving Spirit guide me, always. For all beings who wish to rekindle the flame of love within.

Why are we here, but to open to the beauty?
Why are we here, but to love through the pain?

-"Surrender"
Music by Heather Houston
Lyrics by Samantha Keller

CONTENTS

INTRODUCTION

Mindfulness and compassion practices have changed me. Other beings are no longer my friends or enemies, but mirrors reflecting my spaciousness and limitations. To imagine a different world, I must make space in my heart for all. It's a tall order, but a necessary one. To this end, may these poems inspire us to make space within, so we can meet external chaos and confusion with understanding, with love.

Divine Birth

There's magic in my body,
words swirling in delight,
giddy with the profound realization
that a gush of poetry
is about to enter this world
in wide-eyed wonder,
cradled by those who care.

The Sound of Music

Deep in the heart of Mother Earthrise's
rolling green bosoms,
Bodhisattvas awaken from the slumber of ignorance.

Why do we build walls and bruise egos just to be heard?
Why not listen to the beating of our own heart's rhythm
and sing from this place of self-love?

The world needs confidence, courage, self-compassion
to conquer our mistrust in humanity.

Let the notes punctuate the silent spaces within us
till we are dancing with doubt,
serenading it with our sweet music singing
I am here!
I deserve your love!

Blind

provider, protector
a formidable force
not to be taken lightly

then a softer side
a quivering heart that beats
with the sound of all life

and i see the sacred
masculine and feminine
within him

Bodhicitta
for Mankh

sweet mind
come sit by the heart
there's space for you here

i know you're impatient
i know you want answers

come and just listen
let the heart speak
it was never a race—

for love, and the thought
of love are one in the same

Coming Home

I can't do this anymore,
dance this dance where my heart
is armored, an oyster shell
clammed shut against the soft
meat of what really matters.

I want to know how it is for you,
how the pearl inside is forming
from the irritations of life—
layer upon layer of courage
surrounding the suffering
with warm presence.

Let there be time and space
to show you your pearl
having sat with my own,
cupping my heart in my hands
so I may know yours.

I Have My Mother's Hair

I have my mother's hair, course and curly.
I've wished for smooth and straight
as if hair could be a metaphor
for our relationship—
untangled and straightforward.

I've also inherited her anxiety and
tender compassion for others,
shaping both inside my heart—
journey of acceptance.

I have my mother's hair, course and curly,
the perfect metaphor for a roller coaster ride
where I'm terrified before I get on,
but at the end would still
do it all over again.

She Asked Me

tribute to Pema Chödrön

She asked me to water certain seeds,
to grow kindness and compassion
like wildflowers weathering
any emotional storm.

She asked me to let others die,
to sit in the fires of anger and aversion,
burning all concepts of self
to kill karmic seeds of suffering.

She asked me to soften the scales,
to remember my evolution,
to sit like a buddha on Mother Earth
and rekindle my potential for peace.

The Knot

The knot is not a knot,
but your tangled perception
of what you really want.

If you try and untie it
before its time,
it will only get tighter,
make you more pretzel-like
which no amount of meditation,
massage or yoga can undo.

By year's end
your clenched fist
will become an open palm,
ready for the gift
the knot left behind.

Moment of Truth

We define ourselves by name,
socioeconomic status,
the number of friends on Facebook,
the way our partners look at us,
the extracurricular activities
and colleges our children attend.

What if we lost it all?
Who would we be?
What would we hold onto?

The lunar eclipse is upon us
when the ego,
all black and white thought
can dissolve into the space
of higher consciousness.

The moment of truth has arrived.
Will you become the light?

Embodiment

i am a lotus
in between two worlds
roots anchored in
mud of the underworld
blossom floating on
an ethereal surface
open to Gaia's love

may i bear the balance
of sorrow and joy
suspended between
darkness and light
a bridge of beauty
a symbol of understanding
that it's not possible
to pick sides

Remember

Knock on the door to your heart.
A secret garden awaits you—
plump red strawberries
and wild fragrant jasmine,
a swing where you can fly,
kiss the breeze and
tickle the sun with your toes.

Whoever said there's no such thing
as magic never knew about the door—
how it can open when you need it most,
invite you to play, to rest
to remember the child within—
how she wears a crown of petals
and dances with the wind.

Keeping Time

Be your own keeper of time!
Smash that hourglass,
damn sand never ceasing to fall!

You'll get cut, the bleeding
may not stop for a while.
But it's well worth it—

stepping out of the glass,
sand stretching for miles,
your ocean heart calling

Be who you are meant to me!
Do what you are meant to do!
The tides will be your new rhythm,

and keep time.

Surfing Lesson

Tsunami or swell,
ride your wave
dear one with heart.

No surfing lesson can prepare you
for the journey into a sea of emotions—
the dark soul of the deep.

What if you stepped off the board,
dived way down into the
blue black watery bruises of pain,
stayed for as long as you could
then swam and emerged for air?

What if your breath could save you?
What if you could bathe your
experience in tenderness
and baptize it with love?

Isn't it worth a try?

Breaking the Rules

You don't have to sit like the Tin Man
   rusting,
waiting for someone to lubricate your
joints with the oil of understanding.

You can let your breath
bathe any area of hurt
with blessings of gratitude.
You can make subtle micro-movements,
honoring fluidity over stagnation.

It's not cheating!

I'm sure the Buddha had
well kept secrets
he never shared with the world,
because he wanted each of us
to discover our own divinity
from the inside out—

chair, cushion, bench or floor,
breaking the rules to find
our own heart light.

Forgiveness

Kissed so thoroughly by the sun,
serenaded so sweetly by birdsong,
I've forgotten to ask
What have I done to deserve this?

Maybe the mercy we need most
is from our own inner critics
who just want total acceptance—

forgiveness from a hummingbird,
its iridescent eyes and tireless wings
pausing just long enough
at the bird-feeder to say,

I see you
and I want you to stay
just as you are.

42

I am exactly where I need to be,
not one white hair less,
not one wrinkle more.

Sometimes I think I need to be
more worldly and less serious,
blending in rather than standing out—

abandoning creativity, contemplation
and compassion for a compulsive
inner critic who just wants me to cook,

forgetting that a flame is most
powerful when shining bright
and not just waiting to burn out.

Beyond Character

Compassionate presence is like a stage
supporting all the actors and scenes
long after they're gone.
It doesn't judge which performances
are Broadway worthy or best viewed
at a high school in Nonamesville.

It's the silence between productions
cheering you on at each and every
dress rehearsal, not caring if you
receive a standing ovation
or rotten tomatoes.

It's the space between actors,
an invisible connection between us—
an invitation to meet in the dressing room
out of costumes and makeup
to see who's there.

The Day After

It doesn't have to be so
heavy, loaded
this thing we called life,
a feather yielding,
dancing with the breeze,
floating on incoming tides
to rest at your feet—
a memento you can take
from waves of experience
to remember
the day after the storm.

Emptiness

my cup is empty
waiting to be filled
with the next liquid moment
not knowing what will spill over
what will stay
what will soothe or burn
drinking it all
to be empty once more

Sunday Drive

wild geese flying overhead
a feathery cloud dipped
in the ink of sun colors
Silence asks
Are you paying attention?

Here

It doesn't matter how long you've been gone,
how often you've traveled through
muddy swamps and time machines
as long as you know there's space for you
here in this meditative moment.

The wind can be your worst enemy
or best friend depending on how
you want to breathe and be here—
a being hunted by phantom predators
or gifted with opportunities to awaken.

Still Waiting to Be Written

The only version of you that matters
is your compassionate, present self.
We all want to feel beautiful—
love pouring out of us like rain
ending the drought of disconnection.
We all want to be the star of our show
sans slander against us
face to face or on the internet.
What if connection is not contingent
on approval but compassionate presence?
You don't have to be a book
bound by one particular story,
but several blank pages
still waiting to be written.

Praise and Blame

I don't know who will love me
or hate me in the next moment—
petals strewn across the path
or land mines planted in secret.

It isn't my job to know,
but to walk with an awareness
untainted by any one experience
and a heart still willing to love.

Trust

It isn't something you hold in your hand,
a polished stone you skip across
the surface of Lake Doubt
to reach the other side.

Trust is an open door,
an invisible threshold you cross
without a groom to carry you,
without a spare key.

It's holding your heart in stillness
as it fibrillates wildly with fear,
until it syncs to the sound
of your breath and remembers,

I am exactly where I need to be.
I am safe in this understanding.

In the Stillness

Don't go chasing the horizon
when you can feel the waves beneath you,
the cold wind against your cheek.
Your sailing gypsy heart wants
to capture a sinking sun
when the warmth was always within,
just waiting to be felt
in the stillness after a storm.

Waking Up

When your thoughts are in knots
and your scalp hurts from tension,
it helps to detangle with a comb,
a brush, the breath, this heart.
Only tenderness can separate
the strands of confusion, changing
the to do list into the to be list,
noticing his callused hand on your belly,
firm and reassuring
or the outline of morning light
against the blinds—
a kind invitation to a new day,
a new way of relating to yourself,
the sun rising inside you
to warm the hearts of others.

Together

Let's explore the edges
of our vulnerability together
and not get sucked in its black hole,
holding on to each other's hands,
holding on to each other's hearts
in a circle of endless compassion.

No story is too tragic,
too tender in the light
and space of shared awareness.
It is a novel written by us all—
the chapters changing,
characters, settings, and plots variable.

But suffering is all the same,
believing you are a separate star
when you always belonged
to this solar system—
this darkness, this light.

Visions

Don't look for that half of the moon
lost in shadows.
You'll never find the on switch
to a lamp devoured by darkness.

The half you can see,
the half that matters,
the half that moves tides
of emotion in others,

let this be your third eye
your visions for beauty
your flash of insight
behind cobwebbed clouds.

The world wants full moons
wants to accept you as you are
if you can accept yourself—

phases of you shining,
shadows brought to light.

Cracked Open

This morning the sun was like an egg,
cracked open
against a skillet of blue-gray sky,
spilling secrets of beauty and light
to all who stopped to observe.

What if our hearts were like this—
naked, no boundaries?
Would you be like an egg
risking a fall to break the shell,
to move beyond the armor of fear?

This morning the sun was like an egg,
cracked open,
the yolk of self-compassion
at her center
fueling her love for all.

Heartburn

May I digest each moment with ease,
swallowing slowly ,
just enough fire in the oven
to extract the nutrients
necessary for growth,
expelling the excess,
taking care not to burn others
with blame for my choices—
pausing, sitting, waiting
palms on the heart in prayer
that this practice will lead to peace.

Welcome

Welcome to the Metta retreat.
You are given a Brillo pad
to wipe away the excess grime,
years of accumulated crusting
like barnacles clinging
tightly to a sinking ship.

What are these layers
of unmet expectations
blocking your ability
to love and be loved?
The inquiry is painful,
purposeful, possible.

Taking off rose-colored glasses,
a constricted heart beats freely.
Life is beautiful just as it is.
May this purification be complete.

Alive

the drumming sound of rain
audio cardioversion
her heart beats again

Radiance

lay down your weapons
i didn't come here to fight
i came to witness the unveiling of your heart
a radiant jewel reflecting your True Nature
the nature of all Life
the heart's radiance is its own protection

The Beloved

When I forget,
when the critical voices are louder
than wind chimes, favorite poems
even my own heartbeat,
please help me to remember you—

the way you see me and know exactly
what I need without a single word spoken,
or the way your breath infuses mine with kindness
reaching every cell of my being,
no parts left out.

This is your power,
the power of unconditional, loving presence.
May you never leave me.
May you always love me.
May you know that you are always welcome here.

Testify to Love

You are not your thoughts and emotions.
You are so much more—
an open field of kindness
allowing all that moves through you
ample space to be just as it is,

transforming weeds to wildflowers
marking your sacred path
towards a thinning of the self,
testifying to love with each step
to see the True Nature in all.

Second Chances

raindrop designs
cleared by wipers
new patterns possible

I Will Be There

I am a soothing caress over all your bruises
A fluttering joy in places of ease
I am the first morning light kissing your eyelids
A sliver of moonlight before you enter dark dreams
I am the answer before you ask a question
Unveiled when you are ready to see
I am every boulder and alternate route
A divine flow towards the possibility of awakening
I am a silent presence always with you
Please, oh please my Precious One
Do not travel alone any longer
I will be there when you call my name

Meditation

a gentle breeze
blowing through the heart
sounding chimes of love
what I want to remember most

it doesn't have to be so hard
it can be simple
breathe and music
rocking the body
back and forth

till the rhythm is second nature
till I'm dancing with the Divine

Beyond Intimacy

It's more important to be heard
than to prove a point,
two people unzipping skin
down to soul longing,
down to marrow memories.

He takes off his clothes
but she remains fully dressed,
scared to expose what's underneath.
What if he doesn't like what he sees?
What if she doesn't like what he sees?

He wants something more
beyond skin to skin contact,
beyond what's in a name
to reveal the universe inside him,
to know her space within.

Joy

marshmallow sun melting
in orange-flamed clouds
a delicious day ahead

Daughter

Before you
  I didn't see shades of blue and green—
    turquoise, teal, aquamarine

Before you
  I didn't appreciate messy hair,
    breaking rules, apologies

Before you
  I didn't understand the difference
    between dictators and doormats

Before you
  I didn't have a zafu, an altar
    an undefended heart

Thank you for being my teacher.

Perennial Metta

may we let go of all that is not needed
may we bring kindness to the seed
of our deepest intentions for healing

till the aspirations grow thick
with leaves of longing
withstanding any weather

bearing fruit when we need it most
to taste the truth of the moment
to taste what we have forgotten

A Vase on Display
for MBSM Moms

There is a crack on my backside
against the wall, gathering dust in darkness.
Most people don't even notice it,
choosing to appreciate the polished perfection
of my front side under artificial lights.

But you turn me around,
caressing the crack with your eyes,
soft fingers tracing the journey of fragility,
holding me to wholeness
till I am no longer afraid of breaking.

Stay

It's warm here
Breath against the nostrils
Rise and fall of the chest
Soft belly tensing less
Against the world
One hand holding the other
Wise whisper from with
Beckoning, *Stay*

Sharing the Sky

As he sharpens his intellect
I soften my heart
Afraid to be stabbed multiple times
Afraid of bleeding to death
Will I survive?
Will we survive?

Can we be like sun and moon
Sharing the sky
Meeting at twilight and dawn
Where his brilliance softens
Where moonlight isn't the only
Manifestation of guidance

Where we both flourish
As celestial beings
Sensing sunfire in me
And moondust in you
Expressions of the Universe
Made of the same matter

On Retreat

Each day I light a candle
in your names—
missing you, aching
to know myself,
sitting with the mistakes
and breaths of redemption
as rivulets of tears
flow through the heart,
thankful for the elements
that continue to shape
my love for you
and this life.

Meadow Meditation

for the Kairos House Sangha

Yellow and purple wildflowers grow fearlessly
in the meadow below Kairos House.
What is your secret?, I ask.
Please tell me what you know!
A soft breeze begins their dance—
from tiny seeds of longing,
to sprouts unsure of the weather,
to proud stems blooming blossoms of belonging,
falling one by one to the ground of tomorrow
for the chance to grow again.

Today

Let's make space for each other
on the road, in conversation.
We all want to be seen and heard.
We all want to be the last name
whispered on a loved one's dying lips.
Let's not crowd or cut each other off,
for today might be the last day
we ever meet again.

Stretching the Heart

May my love for you be as wide as the sea—
perpetual ebb and flow of understanding,
riding the incoming tides to kiss your feet,
receding when I am too angry, hurt or scared,
returning with seasoned seashells of love
and the courage to try again.

May I meet these waves with oceanic presence,
rubbing the irritations of life against me
to polish the pearl of knowing
that this overwhelm won't last forever,
that a bead of wisdom is emerging
as a keepsake to remember
it was never about perfection, but presence.

Relationships are beautiful and complex.
We want sweet connections to last.
When we rub each other the wrong way,
may we have the courage to try again.
In doing so, may we stretch our hearts
beyond the boundaries of
greed, hatred, and delusion.

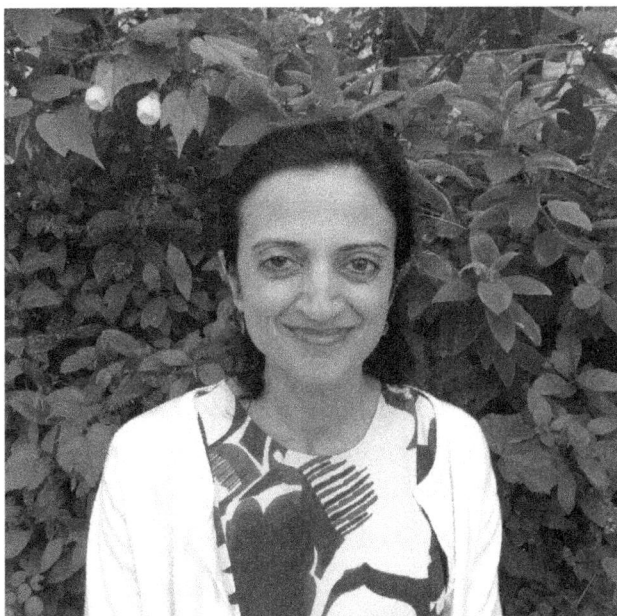

ABOUT THE AUTHOR

Kaveri Patel seeks to initiate meaningful change through fierce, tender presence. Her literary works have appeared in various corners of Earth's eternal heart. Her poetry, publications, and classes can be found at wisdominwaves.com

www.ingramcontent.com/pod-product-compliance
Lightning Source LLC
Chambersburg PA
CBHW030711110426
R18122000001B/R181220PG42736CBX00001B/1